"This guide helped me talk with my doctor after an abnormal test result."

"My doctor explained that cervical cancer screening tests can find changes in cervical cells that can be treated. That was reassuring to know."

"My daughter received the HPV vaccine, so she would be protected. I also learned that my son should be vaccinated."

TABLE OF CONTENTS

Use this guide to learn more and talk with your health care provider about:

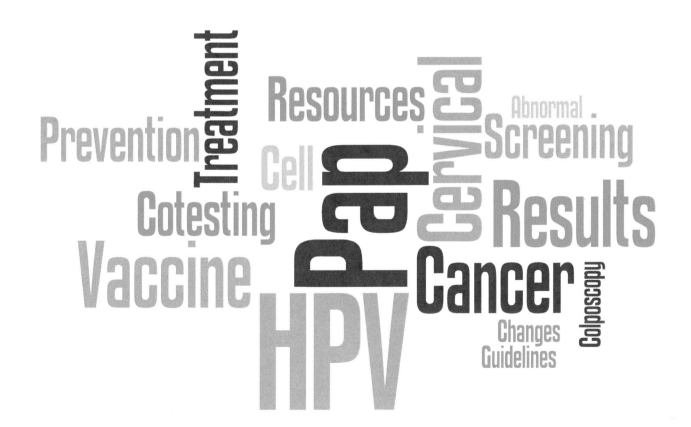

INTRODUCTION

You may be reading this guide because you had an abnormal Pap test or HPV test result. Although it's common to feel uneasy, you should know that most women who have abnormal cervical screening test results do not have cervical cancer. Most have early cell changes that can be monitored (since they often go away on their own) or treated early (to prevent problems later). So, get the follow-up visits, tests, or treatment that your health care provider advises.

Scientific advances have helped us learn much more about how cervical cancer develops, as well as how and when to screen women. However, these advances have also added a layer of complexity for health care providers and women. This guide helps women talk with their health care provider and make informed decisions to prevent cervical cancer.

Good news about preventing cervical cancer

We know what causes cervical cancer.
Nearly all cervical cancer is caused by a virus called HPV (human papillomavirus).

Cervical cell changes happen slowly.
It can take many years for cells infected with HPV to develop into cervical cancer.

We have great tools to prevent cervical cancer.
Cervical cancer screening and early HPV vaccination can prevent cervical cancer.

Better screening tests mean less frequent screening.
Because of improvements in cervical cancer screening, guidelines now recommend less frequent screening than before.

Abnormal test results don't mean that you have cancer.
An abnormal cervical screening test result does not mean that you have cervical cancer. It means that cervical cell changes were found or that cells are infected with HPV. Depending on the results, you may need follow-up testing or treatment. Treatment for cervical changes works well.

HPV INFECTION

"My doctor told me that some types of HPV cause cervical cancer, as well as other types of cancer, even some throat cancers."

HPV (human papillomavirus) and cervical cell changes

HPVs are a group of related viruses, some of which are spread through sexual contact and can cause cancer, including cervical cancer. Here are some basic facts about HPV:

Most HPV infections, even with high-risk types, go away on their own without causing problems. They are fought off by the body's immune system. However, sometimes infections with high-risk HPV types do not go away. When a high-risk HPV infection of cervical cells lasts many years, the cells can become abnormal. These changes can get worse over time and may become cervical cancer. Although there is currently no way to treat an HPV infection, cervical cancer can be prevented by detecting and removing abnormal cervical cells before they become cancer.

HPV infections are common. Most people who are sexually active will have an HPV infection at some point and never know it. HPV infections can be spread through skin-to-skin contact, including vaginal, anal, and oral sex. Although condoms can lower the risk of an HPV infection, they do not protect against them completely.

There are many types of sexually transmitted human papillomaviruses (HPVs).

- High-risk HPV types can infect cervical cells and cause cervical cancer. They can also infect certain other cells to cause anal cancer, penile cancer, vaginal cancer, vulvar cancer, and oropharyngeal cancer (cancer in the middle of the throat, including the tonsils and the back of the tongue).

- Low-risk HPV types can cause genital warts. These are warts on the external and internal sex organs and glands. Genital warts do not turn into cancer.

Smoking may increase the risk that an HPV infection will persist and develop into cervical cancer. So if you smoke and have an abnormal Pap or HPV test result, it is especially important to stop smoking.

PAP TEST AND HPV TEST

"Screening tests can help find cell changes in the cervix early. Sometimes these changes can develop into cancer if they aren't treated."

The Pap test and the HPV test are cervical cancer screening tests.

Screening means checking for disease before there are symptoms. Women need cervical cancer screening even if they feel fine. Screening can help find changes in cervical cells, so you can receive the proper follow-up and treatment you may need, to stay healthy.

The **Pap test** (also called a **Pap smear**) finds cervical cell changes that may turn into cervical cancer. It can also detect cervical cancer cells. A Pap test also sometimes finds conditions, such as infection or inflammation, that are not cancer.

The **human papillomavirus (HPV) test** can find infection with the types of HPV that can cause cancer.

Cotesting means that both the Pap test and the HPV test are done at the same time.

Think you're too busy to get screened for cervical cancer? Think again. Call and make an appointment today.

Clinics that offer screening

Doctors' offices, clinics, and community health centers offer Pap and HPV tests. Many women receive these tests from their ob/gyn (obstetrics/gynecology) doctor. If you don't have a doctor you see regularly you can find a clinic near you that offers cervical cancer screening by contacting:

- your state or local health department

- the National Breast and Cervical Cancer Early Detection Program (NBCCEDP) of the Centers for Disease Control and Prevention (CDC) at 1-800-232-4636 or www.cdc.gov

- a Planned Parenthood clinic at 1-800-230-7526 or www.plannedparenthood.org

What to expect

Cervical cancer screening tests are usually done during a pelvic exam. During this exam, you lie on your back on an exam table, bend your knees, and put your feet into stirrups. The health care provider gently opens your vagina with a speculum to see the cervix. A soft, narrow brush or spatula is used to collect a small sample of cells from your cervix.

The sample of cervical cells is sent to the lab and checked for any abnormal cervical cells. The same sample can also be checked for HPV, with an HPV test. When both a Pap test and an HPV test are done, this is called cotesting.

A pelvic exam includes more than just taking samples for a Pap and/or HPV test. Your health care provider will also check the size, shape, and position of the uterus and ovaries and feel for any lumps or cysts. The rectum may also be checked for lumps or abnormal areas. Most health care providers will tell you what to expect at each step of the exam, so you will be at ease. When you talk with your health care provider, you may also ask to be tested for sexually transmitted infections (STIs).

Questions to ask before and after your exam

Before your exam

Ask your health care provider:

- What will happen during the exam?
- What tests will I have and why?
- Will I have any discomfort?

Your health care provider may ask you:

- What was the start date of your last period?
- When did you have your last Pap and/or HPV test?
- What were your test results?

After your exam

Ask your health care provider:

- When will I get my test results?
- How will I get these results (e.g., by mail or a phone call)?
- What phone number should I call if I do not get my test results?
- When I get my results, will they explain what I should do next?

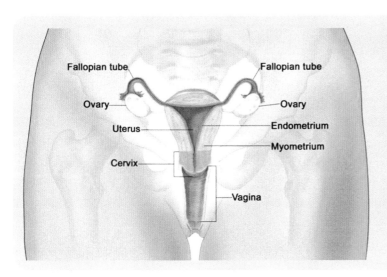

The female reproductive system

The cervix is part of the female reproductive system. It's the lower, narrow end of the uterus, which leads to the vagina, as shown in the image above. The cervix opens during childbirth to allow the baby to pass.

SCREENING GUIDELINES: WHEN TO GET SCREENED

Cervical cancer screening guidelines for most women

Cervical cancer screening recommendations have been updated by the United States Preventive Services Task Force (USPSTF) (www.uspreventiveservicestaskforce.org) and other organizations, based on:

- Research showing that HPV-caused changes in cervical cells happen slowly and often go away on their own, especially in younger women

- More effective screening tests

- Research showing the harms of overtesting and overtreatment for cervical changes that would have gone away on their own

"Talk with your health care provider to find out how often to have cervical cancer screening. The guidelines have recently changed."

Talk with your health care provider about when to start screening, how often to be screened, and what screening test to have. These ages and times between screenings apply to most women, as long as they have normal test results. The guidelines do not apply to women with certain medical conditions, as noted in the box on page 5.

"My patients who are over 30 years old can get both the Pap and HPV tests together. This is called cotesting. It means they may only need to be screened every 5 years, as long as their test results are normal."

Age 21 years

Women should get their first Pap test at age 21. Even if a woman is already sexually active, Pap tests are not recommended until the age of 21.

Age 21-29 years

Pap testing every 3 years is recommended for women in their 20s. Women in this age group should not have routine HPV testing because HPV infections at these ages tend to last only a short time before going away by themselves. However, if a woman in this age group has an abnormal Pap test result, follow-up testing may include an HPV test.

Age 30-65 years

It is recommended that women in this age group get both a Pap test and an HPV test (called cotesting) every 5 years or a Pap test alone every 3 years. This longer interval still allows cell changes to be detected in time to treat them if needed but reduces treatment of cell changes that would go away on their own anyway.

Older than 65 years

Women in this age group should talk with their health care provider to learn if screening is still needed. If you have been screened regularly and your recent test results have been normal, your health care provider will probably advise you that you no longer need screening. However, if your recent test results were abnormal or if you have not been screened regularly, it is important to talk with your health care provider about screening.

Exceptions to the guidelines

Depending on your medical history, your health care provider may recommend more or less frequent screening.

More frequent screening may be recommended for women who:

- are HIV positive
- have a weakened immune system
- were exposed before birth to a medicine called diethylstilbestrol (DES), which was once prescribed to pregnant women
- had a recent abnormal Pap test or biopsy result
- have had cervical cancer

Screening is not needed for women who:

- have had a hysterectomy for reasons not related to cancer or cervical cell changes. However, if your hysterectomy was related to cervical cancer, talk with your health care provider to learn what follow-up care you need.

PAP TEST RESULTS

Pap test results show if cervical cells are normal or abnormal. A Pap test may also come back as unsatisfactory.

Next steps after a Pap test may include:

Normal Pap test results: Your health care provider will usually recommend another screening exam in 3 to 5 years. A normal test result may also be called a **negative test result**.

Unsatisfactory Pap test results: Your health care provider will ask you to come in for another Pap test. The lab sample may not have had enough cells, or the cells may have been clumped together or hidden by blood or mucus.

Abnormal Pap test results: Your health care provider will recommend more testing or treatment for these findings: **ASC-US, AGC, LSIL, ASC-H, HSIL**, or **AIS**. These cervical cell changes are listed in the table, on the next page, in order from less serious to more serious. These changes may be referred to as dysplasia, neoplasia, or precancer – cells that are abnormal, but are not cancer. An abnormal test result may also be called a **positive test result**.

"Need help understanding your test results? Ask your health care provider what your test results mean and what you should do next."

Pap test results usually come back from the lab in about 1-3 weeks. You may receive a letter or a phone call from your health care provider. If you don't hear from your provider, call and ask for your test results. Ask about any follow-up visits or tests you may need.

More about biopsy findings and CIN

CIN is also called **cervical intraepithelial neoplasia**. This means that abnormal cells were found on the surface of the cervix. CIN is usually caused by certain types of human papillomavirus (HPV) and is found when a cervical biopsy is done. **CIN is not cancer**, but may become cancer and spread to nearby normal tissue if not treated. It is graded on a scale of 1 to 3, based on how abnormal the cells look under a microscope and how much of the cervical tissue is affected. For example, CIN 1 has slightly abnormal cells and is less likely to become cancer than CIN 2 or CIN 3.

Pap test results and possible next steps

ASC-US **Atypical Squamous Cells of Undetermined Significance**	**ASC-US** is the most common abnormal Pap test finding. It means that some cells don't look completely normal, but it's not clear if the changes are caused by HPV infection. Other things can cause cells to look abnormal, such as irritation, some infections, such as a yeast infection, growths such as polyps or cysts that are benign (not cancer), and changes in hormones that occur during pregnancy or menopause. Although these things may make cervical cells look abnormal, they are not related to cancer. **Possible next steps:** An HPV test is usually done, or the Pap test may be repeated in 12 months.
AGC **Atypical Glandular Cells**	**AGC** means that some glandular cells were found that do not look normal. More testing is usually recommended. **Possible next steps:** Colposcopy and biopsy. See the Follow-up Testing section on page 10 to learn about these procedures.
LSIL **Low-Grade Squamous Intraepithelial Lesions**	**LSIL** is sometimes called mild dysplasia. It may also be called CIN 1. LSIL means that there are low-grade changes. LSIL changes are usually caused by HPV infection. Although the changes may go away on their own, further testing is usually done to find out whether there are more severe changes that need to be treated. **Possible next steps:** Colposcopy and biopsy. See the Follow-up Testing section on page 10 to learn about these procedures.
ASC-H **Atypical Squamous Cells, Cannot Exclude HSIL**	**ASC-H** means that some abnormal squamous cells were found that may be a high-grade squamous intraepithelial lesion (HSIL), although it's not certain. More testing is recommended. **Possible next steps:** Colposcopy and biopsy. See the Follow-up Testing section on page 10 to learn about these procedures.
HSIL **High-Grade Squamous Intraepithelial Lesions**	**HSIL** is sometimes called moderate or severe dysplasia. It may also be called CIN 2, CIN 2/3, or CIN 3. HSIL means that there are more serious changes than LSIL, in cervical cells. These changes are caused by HPV and may turn into cervical cancer if not treated. **Possible next steps:** Colposcopy and biopsy. See the Follow-up Testing section on page 10 to learn about these procedures.
AIS **Adenocarcinoma In Situ**	**AIS** means that an advanced lesion (area of abnormal growth) was found in the glandular tissue of the cervix. AIS lesions may become cancer (cervical adenocarcinoma) if not treated. **Possible next steps:** Colposcopy and biopsy. See the Follow-up Testing section on page 10 to learn about these procedures.
Cervical Cancer Cells	Sometimes cervical cancer cells (squamous cell carcinoma or adenocarcinoma) are found. However, for women who are screened at regular intervals, it is very rare for cancer cells to be found on a Pap test. For more information about cervical cancer, call 1-800-4-CANCER (1-800-422-6237) or visit www.cancer.gov/cervical. **Possible next steps:** Colposcopy and biopsy. See the Follow-up Testing section on page 10 to learn about these procedures.

Cervical changes

These images show how cervical cells that have long-lasting infections with high-risk HPV can change over time and become abnormal. Abnormal cervical cells may also return to normal even without treatment, especially in younger women. LSIL and HSIL are two types of abnormal changes to cervical squamous cells.

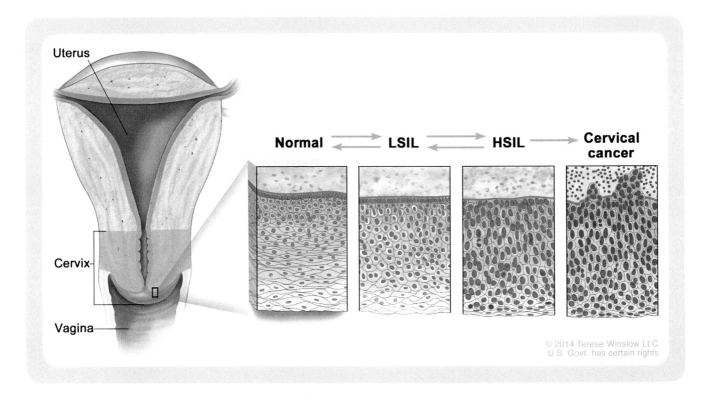

COTESTING RESULTS

"My doctor told me how the Pap test and HPV test work. She took the time to help me understand the next steps and why I needed to take them."

If you get both a Pap and an HPV test, this is called **cotesting**. The guidelines advise that routine Pap and HPV cotesting be limited to women age 30 and older. However, HPV testing can be used in women of any age after an unclear Pap test finding and to help your health care provider determine if further evaluation is needed.

Your cotest results were normal

Pap test result (normal) and HPV test result (normal)
If both your Pap test and your HPV test results are normal, your health care provider will probably tell you that you can wait 5 years before your next cotest (Pap and HPV test).

Your cotest results came back abnormal

Pap test result (normal) and HPV test result (abnormal)
Your health care provider will probably recommend that you come back for repeat cotesting in 12 months or have a different HPV test.

Pap test result is (abnormal) and HPV test result is (normal)
- **For abnormal Pap test result of ASC-US:** Most women are advised to get another Pap and HPV test in 3-5 years.
- **For all other abnormal Pap test results:** Your health care provider will probably recommend that you come in for a test called a colposcopy, which is used to take a closer look at your cervix and perform a biopsy. Based on the colposcopy findings, your health care provider will decide whether further testing or treatment is needed.

Pap test result (abnormal) and HPV test result (abnormal)
When both the Pap test and the HPV test results are abnormal, you will need further testing and possibly treatment. The first step is usually a colposcopy. A colposcopy is an exam that allows your health care provider to take a closer look at your cervix and to remove a sample of cervical cells for a pathologist to examine; this procedure is called a biopsy. The sample is then checked under a microscope for signs of disease. Based on the results, your health care provider will decide whether further testing or treatment is needed.

Learn more about Pap Test Results on page 6 **and about** Follow-up Testing on page 10.

About HPV testing alone for cervical cancer screening

Recent research findings indicate that the HPV test alone is highly effective for cervical cancer screening. The FDA recently approved this use. In the future, cervical screenings may only require an HPV test instead of a cotest. Talk with your healthcare provider to learn more.

FOLLOW-UP TESTING

Keep in mind that most women with abnormal cervical screening test results do not have cancer. However, if you have an abnormal test result, it's important to get the follow-up tests and/or treatment that your health care provider recommends. Possible next steps and treatments are listed in this section to help you learn more and talk with your health care provider.

"My doctor told me that my abnormal test result didn't mean that I have cancer. Now that was a relief to hear."

Depending upon your test result, next steps may include:

Pap test: Some women may need to return for another Pap test.

HPV test: An HPV test may be recommended.

Estrogen cream: If you have ASC-US and are near or past menopause, your health care provider may prescribe estrogen cream. If the cell changes are caused by low hormone levels, applying estrogen cream will make them go away.

Colposcopy and biopsy: Your health care provider will examine your cervix using a colposcope and perform a biopsy. A colposcopy is a procedure to examine your cervix. During this procedure, your doctor inserts a speculum to gently open the vagina and see the cervix. Diluted white vinegar is put on the cervix, causing abnormal areas to turn white. Your doctor then places an instrument called a colposcope close to the vagina. It has a bright light and a magnifying lens and allows your doctor to look closely at your cervix.

A colposcopy usually includes a biopsy. A biopsy is done so that the cells or tissues can be checked under a microscope for signs of disease. In addition to removing a sample for further testing, some types of biopsies may be used as treatment, to remove abnormal cervical tissue or lesions.

Types of cervical biopsies include:

- **Endocervical curettage**: cells are scraped from the lining of the cervical canal

- **Punch biopsy**: a small piece of cervical tissue is removed

- **Cone biopsy** (or **conization**): a cone-shaped sample of cervical tissue is removed

Talk with your doctor to learn what to expect during and after your procedure. Some women have bleeding and/or discharge after a biopsy. Others have pain that feels like menstrual cramps. The questions below may be helpful as you talk with your health care provider to learn more.

Questions to ask before a test or procedure

- What is the purpose of this test or procedure? _____

  _____

- What will the results tell us?_____

  _____

- What will happen during the procedure? _____

  _____

- How long will the procedure take?_____

- Should I limit any activities after the procedure? For how long?_____

  _____

- What problems or side effects should I call you about after the procedure? _____

  _____

TREATMENTS FOR CERVICAL CELL CHANGES

Some abnormal cervical changes need to be removed so they do not turn into cancer. Your doctor will talk with you about which treatment is recommended for you and why. The questions at the end of this section can help you talk with your health care provider to learn more.

"It was reassuring to talk with my doctor. She helped me understand what to expect. It was comforting to learn how this treatment would help me."

Common treatment methods include:

Cold knife conization (also called **cold knife cone biopsy**) is a procedure in which a cone-shaped piece of abnormal tissue is removed from the cervix using a scalpel or laser knife. Some of the tissue is then checked under a microscope for signs of disease, such as cervical cancer. This procedure is done at the hospital and requires general anesthesia.

Cryotherapy is a procedure in which an extremely cold liquid or an instrument called a cryoprobe is used to freeze and destroy abnormal tissue. A cryoprobe is cooled with substances such as liquid nitrogen, liquid nitrous oxide, or compressed argon gas. Also called cryoablation and cryosurgery. This procedure is done in your doctor's office. It takes only a few minutes and usually does not require anesthesia.

Laser therapy is a procedure that uses a laser (narrow beam of intense light) to destroy abnormal tissue. This procedure is done at the hospital and general anesthesia is used.

LEEP (loop electrosurgical excision procedure) is a procedure in which a thin wire loop, through which an electrical current is passed, to remove abnormal tissue. Local anesthesia is used to numb the area. Your doctor usually performs this procedure in the office. It takes only a few minutes, and you will be awake during the procedure.

Questions to ask before treatment

- What are the possible treatments for the condition that I have? _____
  _____
  _____

- What are the advantages and disadvantages of each treatment?_____
  _____
  _____

- Which treatment do you recommend for me, and why? _____
  _____
  _____

- What will happen during the treatment?_____
  _____
  _____

- What are the possible risks of this treatment? _____
  _____
  _____

- How might this treatment affect a future pregnancy? _____
  _____
  _____

- How long will the procedure take? _____
  _____
  _____

- Will general or local anesthesia be needed? _____
  _____
  _____

- What side effects might I have from this procedure? _____
  _____
  _____

- How long might these side effects last? _____
  _____
  _____

- Are there any activities that I should avoid after the procedure? _____
  _____
  _____

HPV VACCINATION

Human papillomavirus (HPV) vaccination protects against infection with HPV types that cause:

- nearly all cases of cervical cancer

- most cases of anal cancer and many cases of penile cancer, vaginal cancer, vulvar cancer, and oropharyngeal cancer (cancers of the throat, tongue, tonsils, and soft palate).

HPV vaccination also protects against infection by the HPV types that cause most warts on or around the genitals and anus.

"Visit your local clinic or call your child's doctor to learn how the HPV vaccine can protect your son or daughter."

Answers to commonly asked questions:

At what age, should children get the HPV vaccine?
Girls and boys should start the HPV vaccine series at age 11 or 12; it may be started at age 9 and given through age 26. Preteens often receive the HPV vaccine at the same time as the whooping cough and meningitis vaccines. Preteens have a stronger immune response to the HPV vaccine than older adolescents.

How many doses are given?
Under the age of 15: Two doses of the vaccine are given. The second dose is given 6-12 months after the first dose.

Ages 15-26: Three doses of the vaccine are given. The second dose is given 1-2 months after the first dose, and the third dose is given 6 months after the first dose.

What if someone didn't get the recommended doses at a younger age or complete the series?
Vaccination can be given up to age 26 if necessary to complete the series.

Do vaccinated women still need to be screened for cervical cancer?
Yes. Because HPV vaccination doesn't protect against all HPV types that can cause cervical cancer, it's important to get regular screening.

Is the HPV vaccine safe?
Yes. Side effects of the HPV vaccine are similar to those of other vaccines and may include mild pain in the arm where the vaccine was given. Sometimes a slight fever, dizziness, or nausea may also occur.

What impact has HPV vaccination had so far?
Infection with HPV types targeted by the vaccine has gone down substantially among teenage girls since vaccination was recommended in the U.S. (HPV Infections Targeted by Vaccine Decrease in U.S.)

RELATED RESOURCES

"Call or go online to learn more about cervical cancer prevention and screening from these organizations."

National Cancer Institute (NCI)

NCI has comprehensive research-based information on cervical cancer prevention, screening, diagnosis, treatment, genetics and supportive care. Our information specialists can answer your questions and help you find information. You can contact us by phone, online chat, or e-mail.

1-800-422-6237 (1-800-4-CANCER)
www.cancer.gov or www.cancer.gov/espanol
livehelp.cancer.gov (online chat)
cancergovstaff@mail.nih.gov (email)
https://go.usa.gov/x59au (Promotional Flyer for Health Professionals to Give to Women)
www.cancer.gov/cervical (Cervical Cancer Home Page)

Agency for Healthcare Research and Quality (AHRQ)

The United States Preventive Services Task Force (USPSTF), convened by the AHRQ, uses a rigorous process to develop recommendations for many preventive interventions, including cervical cancer screening.

1-301-427-1104
www.uspreventiveservicestaskforce.org

Centers for Disease Control and Prevention (CDC)

The CDC's National Breast and Cervical Cancer Early Detection Program (NBCCEDP) helps women who have low income or do not have health insurance get Pap tests, pelvic exams, diagnostic tests, and referrals. The CDC website also has information about the human papillomavirus (HPV).

1-800-232-4636 (1-800-CDC-INFO)
www.cdc.gov

National Library of Medicine (NLM)

MedlinePlus is the NLM's site for patients and their families and friends. It has information about HPV and other cervical cancer screening-related topics, including the latest treatments, medical videos, and links to medical research.

1-888-346-3656 (1-888-FIND-NLM)
https://medlineplus.gov

Scan this QR code to see an online or
e-book version of this publication:

Or visit us online at
www.cancer.gov/ucc

NIH Publication No. 17-5199
May 2017

Made in the USA
Columbia, SC
08 September 2020